Obeying the Call

Ray Liversidge

Obeying the Call

GINNINDERRA PRESS

Acknowledgements

Some of these poems, or earlier versions of them,
have appeared in the following journals:

Antipodes (USA), *ars poetica*, *ArtStreams*,
Australian Multicultural Book Review, *Brisbane Courier Mail*,
bystander, *Canberra Times*, *Centoria*, *Coppertales*, *Divan*,
The Famous Reporter, *fourWten:carp*, *Gathering Force*, *Heartland*,
Hobo, *Jones Ave* (Canada), *Kangaroo*, *Lip Service*, *Moments*, *Muse*,
New Writing, *Nocturnal Submissions*, *Northern Perspective*,
Obscure Realms, *OZpoet* website, *The Ordinary Magic* (NZ), *Pelt*,
Poetry Australia, *Poetry Monash*, *Poetry on Paper*, *Pook*, *Redoubt*,
Rocky Hill Lines, *Sextuality Anthology*, *SideWaLK*, *Small Packages*,
The Small Times, *Spindrift*, *The Subterranean*, *Swyntax*,
Sydney Morning Herald, *Ulitarra*, *Valley Voices*, *Verso*, *Westerly*.

Ray Liversidge is available for readings.
Festival organisers and other interested groups
can e-mail him: rayliversidge@hotmail.com

Dedicated to my children:
Sarah, Caitlin and Reuben

First published 2003 by
GINNINDERRA PRESS
PO Box 53 Charnwood ACT 2615
www.ginninderrapress.com.au

Printed by Pirion, Fyshwick, ACT

Contents

1

Animal Farm

The company of spiders

The spider finds a home
on the kitchen window sill

suspended among glass
bottles and jars.

A mandala pregnant with meaning
she squats and waits –

her back bubbling with unborn babies.
By morning her children are leaving

the dead body and moving out
from the centre of the web

along delicate threads
to the circle's rim.

'You can't just leave them there!'
my daughter protests,

arms flailing, hands flapping;
while her brother suggests

flushing them down the sink.
As the children ready for school

I take the jar outside,
place it in the garden

amongst fallen bark and snowgrass,
and linger in the company of spiders.

Blackbirds & nightingales

1.

the pressure
finally

too much
to bear

together we
seek relief

return
without a word

to the cold
comfort of bed

resuming
spoony postures

in the dark
I lie awake

listening to
the slow

diminuendo
of chthonic water

is that your stomach
or is it mine?

the earth turns
on its side

and answers
with a sigh

blinded to
the view I have

not of stars
bedimmed by apathy

but a galaxy
obscenely meretricious

a moon lewd
with light

culpably silent

2.

wasted by wine
and talk

we sought
solace in bed

forgetting beauty
in pursuit of truth

I found only truth
without charity

mea culpa

3.

and now
as light

falls in
the space

between their
moony shapes

she wakes and
begins to weep

as he cries himself
to sleep

to dream
of nightingales

when blackbirds
are warbling

in the morning heat

This & that

With stately elegance
    The cat sits on my lap;
Exchanging a casual glance
    We return with insouciance –
Me to this, her to that.

Blackbirds & nightingales 2

1.

You sought the strong and silent type,
I played the victim to your stalking beauty;

And when I thought we'd found
The words to say to one another

Your kisses took my breath away,
Your mouth unmanned me in the dark.

For years we slept supinely in our bed,
And blamed each other when we didn't wake.

2.

Born from the knocking dark,
The silent, bloody theatre of expression,

This morning brings birds in quick propinquity
To roost upon a sapling's votive branch;

Their presence more vivid than
Any dream, bright as this love

Which asks only that we kiss,
And call each other by our names.

Passing through Bubastis

for Brian

... And it's the sudden appearance of your face
at the kitchen window at feeding time
I remember most of all. Feeding time
which, for you, was any time between sunrise
and the moment the lights went out in the house
in the evening. Now your time has come,
and the light in your cold, uncaring eyes is gone.
And still your bowl remains outside the door,
the scene of ceaseless insect activity: ants,
flies, fleas. Especially the ants which run
in dark electric lines around the rim
to form a perfect figure eight. And that's eight
to go – lives, that is. Another eight
before the native birds can sing again
and smaller creatures move more freely through
the grass.

You were useful once inside
the granaries of Egypt – but that was long ago
and times have changed. You serve no purpose now.
And when you died you weren't embalmed
or buried in a cemetery; instead,
my daughter's children asked to put the body in
a cardboard box and place it in the garden.

I try and get out now and then
and spend some time sweeping leaves
or caring for the flower bed...
until my daughter calls me
to come inside and eat.

The death of a bird

At that moment only the mind survives
to make the final flight to silent skies;

the rest's reduced to dross:
a shock of feathers, skin and bone

affixed like scales to the body
of some extinct reptile...

And yet how one wing appears
to resist the passing cars

and beat against the wind
in another flight of fancy.

Feathers

Instead of party lights you hang
Bright orange feathers (from a boa?)
Around the veranda. A feather
For each of your thirty seven years?
No. For all those people in you life,
You say, both past and present.
While my youngest daughter waits in
The car, your son asks you to point
To the feather which is his daddy.
Some things go the way of the dodo -
Doomed to failure, a flightless life.
Feathers are for flying, I yell, waving
You farewell, freefalling into the night...
Not thinking of someone else.

Animal farm

The farm of old McDonald
Is in our bed this morning.
All manner of bird and beast
Running riot. Last night all was quiet,
Quiet as a mouse: with a squeak
Squeak here, small talk there,
And awkward silence everywhere.
I watch a chicken de-clucked by
A fox's presence, find a real frog
Drowning in an imaginary pond.
Now the sun rises on our nakedness -
The cock that doesn't crow a silent
Reminder from a recent dunghill,
Then the shrill entropy of birdsong.

2

Sex

Pornography

Two of Indonesia's three species of tigers have become extinct and the
third is threatened because of the belief that tiger parts can improve
sexual performance.
– The *Age*, 3/1/1997

O tiger! Tonight
my forest is burning from
your mortal eye, your mortal hand.

Claw my shoulder.
Can you feel my heart?
Let me lick the furnace of your feet.

Tiger, where's the hammer?
Hang on… I'll get the chains.
I have to have the anvil of your love.

What? Try the near-
deadly clasp of collar?
Dare me begat a watery heaven?

O tiger, you're nothing but a lamb!
Here, take this. It's better than Viagra.
Now, give it to me tiger – all seven seconds of it.

Sweet dreams, baby

Why keep a pad
   And pen beside your bed
To note the dreams
   Inside your head?
I think some things
   Are better left unsaid,
Some things
   Are better left in bed.

Dreams are dreams
   And nothing more,
Just mental junk
   Left on the floor;
And there's no key
   That unlocks the door –
Some things in life
   One should ignore.

There, let me put
   The pad and pen aside
So you can come
   And sit beside
Your dad and play
   A game we haven't tried.
That's my little girl –
   Now open wide.

An echo ends
   Where it begins
My one and only
   Darling cherubim;
So if I leave
   Every now and then
It doesn't mean I won't
   Be back again.

When all is said
   (And all is done)
Love lies in wait
   For everyone;
So lie and wait
   For me to come,
And dream about me
   While I'm gone.

Fugue with Coda

Subject

The spirit was willing but there was something wrong with the
flesh
He rolled off and onto his back
She said what's wrong
He said nothing
He turned his head and looked at his shoulder to see if a little
angelic figure was sitting there
She thought he was looking at her and stifled a yawn
Damn he thought damn conscience

Prelude

She was a friend of his daughter who he had met one afternoon
after school
Dad this is Natalie
Hello Natalie
Natalie would like to borrow one of your books on poetry for an
assignment
Oh really which one
Any of these poets dad she said handing him a list
He looked at Natalie before perusing the bookshelf
And maybe you could help her choose a topic
He took down the collected works of Dylan Thomas and
suggested loss of innocence as a topic

Subject (Return)

He felt his cock
Still limp
He asked why and a voice in his right ear said because she's half
as old as you and the same age your wife was when you first
made love to her
She said what's wrong
He said why do you young people mutilate yourselves with body
piercing
I said she have to go
Oh by the way said he what mark did you get for your
assignment

Coda

She went home lay on the bed and looking up at the poster of the
all boy pop group on the wall slowly slipped two fingers into
herself
He got up from his bed and standing in front of the mirror took
his hardened cock in his hand

A tongue

can do
what a cock
cannot

bring a bud
to flower
in darkness

A change in the weather

I tell her the problem appears to be
In that area there where a trough of low pressure extends
From the Great Dividing Range to the low centred near Tasmania.
Placing her hand on mine
She says she can feel high pressure systems
Moving in from the Bight and the Tasman Sea.
Dripping with perspiration I ask her
If she thinks conditions are likely to remain humid.
Slowly removing her designer T-shirt and skirt
To reveal the latest in two-piece swimwear
She answers that circumstances will remain unchanged
While pressures continue to be exerted in certain places.
Falling back onto my towel I question her about the future.
She says the forecast is for more unstable weather
With the possibility of a late thunderstorm.
And then without warning she leans across and tracing
The outline of my bathers with her finger
Whispers in my ear something about isobars and suggests
That if I don't like the weather at the moment to wait
And it will almost certainly change.

Reading the signs

One kiss, one speech, one touch, one fuck:
These things alone do not a conflict solve.
One act of clumsy love cannot console
The heart while hands lay idle in the dark.

One repentant speech does not make up
For silent days when mouths were twisted in resolve.
One kiss, one speech, one touch, one fuck:
These things alone do not a conflict solve.

One lingering kiss will not do much
To satisfy the lips if tales remain untold.
And then in times of need you hold

My hand while I cry out, 'That's not enough.'
One kiss, one speech, one touch, one fuck:
These things alone do not a conflict solve.

Synchronicity (Or, Fancy meeting you here)

Between drinks and jokes I'm transfixed
By your hypnotic gazes.
Naturally, I take it as a sign
That a platonic phase is
Made redundant by those looks, and so begin
To shout Byronic phrases
To win your heart and maybe lose myself
In the more erotic places
Of your anatomy.

Captivated by your smile
I take a few chaotic paces
(Leaving the boys behind to dream
Of wild exotic chases)
And make my way amongst the crowd
To where the narcotic haze is
Thickest. And so, as our bodies move closer,
The eyes in our myopic faces
Meet... In the morning we'll try and
Fill in those mnemonic spaces
In our aching heads; but for now it's off to the conjugal bed
On the usual symbiotic basis.

Friday night at the Apollo Milk Bar

It seems the boys are blessed
with serendipity tonight
and celebrate their joy
by sucking on a can of Coke,
lighting up another cigarette,
striking macho poses to shame
even the most curious animal.
For, out of school uniform,
she is Aphrodite in denim,
Madonna in underwear...
any fantasy they want her to be
on this warm November evening.

After placing her order she sits
To wait at the green laminex table.
Through the last O of APOLLO
she notices the older boy in the group
is watching her from the street
while the others cough, guffaw,
and plot in crude and broken English
to do the things that boys are wont to do
at the Apollo Milk Bar after dark.

From the doorway a hand brushes aside
plastic strips; a foot pirouettes
on the linoleum (she feels they see
the sudden shaping in the leg);
then she twists, and turns her back on the boys
and walks towards the corner and the waiting car:
the taste of vanilla milk shake in her mouth,
the fried fat of chips on her smiling lips.
As the car disappears into the night
she lets her body slide down the back seat,
satisfied that she has left them
wondering if it was a wave of the hand
they saw through the rear window
or the head of a toy dog nodding.

Love hurts

Some say I took it from my bag,
And holding it up for him to see
Said something about love,
Then ran the blade along my cheek
Before he had a chance to act.

Others thought they saw me lift
The knife, say something about love,
Then try to slash his handsome face.
He grabbed my hand and bent it back –
And that was when my cheek was cut.

Then there are those who swear
They saw him reach inside his jacket,
And heard him threaten to disfigure me
If love was mentioned once again.
Then his hand was seen to move
Toward my face with something in it.

I admit I can't remember everything
About the party. They say I seemed
A bit on edge that night; and I guess
I smoked and drank a bit too much
To try and calm my nerves.
Yet everyone agreed they'd never seen
Me dance so much and have such fun.
If I no longer laugh it's because
I miss his touch upon my cheek…
And live with the thought of forever bearing
This long and lovely reminder of his smile.

A valediction: forbidding sex

On the first night I sang
some songs of John Donne
and spoke on the metaphysics of love...
but she said that I would say and do
almost anything just to get her into bed.
Last night I read to her from
'The Love Song of J. Alfred Prufrock'...
but she accused me of sexual harassment.
Tonight I tried a canto of Pound:
Pull down thy pantihose
I said pull down...
Instead, she slapped my face,
kicked me in the groin,
and left the house calling me
a crazy gender fascist.

Sex

you can
catch them
at any party
picnic
pub or
barbecue
hunting
in packs
of four
or five
or more
like dogs
seeking safety
in numbers
strength in
sex

3

Reef Dreaming

To rhyme with water

If I suggest the beach
is within reach
she says the sea sux.
The local pool?
Uncool.
And when, in anger, I mention
a river near Phoenix…
Well, it's then she begins to cry.
So I drive to a lake in Ballarat
where she quickly runs to a tree
and hides her face in the shade.
After a long silence she walks
down to the water's edge
where I motion her to come in
as I need her
to rhyme with water.
Tossed pebbles summon
rock wood water
then the sound of laughter circling the lake
before breaking at her feet.
'In your face, Dad!'

As day drifts into evening
she comes and sits beside me
on the bank, her hair wet
and dark against the pale skin.
We look at each other,
the pile of pebbles in her palm:
vocables: cool, wicked.

Not waving

She enters the wat-
er. Waves curl like rice-paper
in the pale moonlight.

Two fishermen

by the north side
of the mountain
on the south bank
of the river
an angler dreams –
his line held in
the light of the moon
moves from side to side
like a trout swimming

by the south side
of the mountain
on the north bank
of the river
an angler casts
his line into the sun –
it arcs in the air
like a trout leaping

Ash Wednesday

> ... I made the nights
> resound in silence with remembered loving
> yet lost you in the grinding daily chores.
> – Bruce Beaver

1.

Summer comes around
soon enough – the next
bend in fact: the familiar

shoulder of the hill
dipping into surf,
the flank bright with the sun

of the very first day,
and the family cabin
(like a postcard)

tucked into the gap
between
forest and sea.

2.

The car turns onto the Great Ocean Road.
He's decided he should drive,
so she sits on the side of the forest.

The holiday has ended as it began –
with whimpering children and the fly-wire
door banging against the jamb.

In Anglesea she notices a house
which wasn't there last year…and sees
young lovers running into the water

hand in hand or walking in the woods
at dusk, the trunks of trees flushed
with light, the leaves thick and shaking

with the *frisson* of stolen moments. Now
days distend with daily chores, while nights
rebound in silence with remembered loving.

'I said it has to be inside the car.'
The lights change at Moorabool Street
as her mind goes back to the forest.

'I spy with my little eye something beginning with f.'
As he did on the trip up, the father
points out the flame at the oil refinery.

On the outskirts of Melbourne she sees the bare
branches, follows the line of the eucalypt
and finds the fern, its frond unfurling from blackness.

Doing a Keats/doing a Shelley

for Mark O'Connor

You turn on the TV and there he is
doing a Keats in your living room:
sitting under a mango tree writing
not about the song of the nightingale
or blustery westerly winds,
but of herons moving silently among mangrove swamps
and underwater worlds of reef and polyp.
In this part of the country
there are no unheard voices to trouble the waters
or evoke a flight to an imaginary land.
Here, the birds are real and the land is real,
and, I suppose, nothing else really matters.
You flick the switch thinking he's gone...
but find him still there, now doing a Shelley:
being washed ashore on the kitchen floor
with a book of poems in his clammy hand.

Whales

By now
I'm usually halfway
along the road
– the shouting over,
the crying done –
and about to turn
back to the house
to say sorry again
when the familiar notes
of Carole King's piano
float from your bedroom window
and drift across the bay
like yachts before the wind…
But it's too late, now darling,
it's too late…

This time
I continue to
the end of the road
until I reach the bluff.
Below, whales,
like spent emotions, beached
and breathless on the sand.

Reef dreaming

for Sarah

Leaving the boat
you enter the world of water
naked of knowledge –
schooled only in the use
of snorkel, mask and flipper.
At first, uncertain of the ocean's depth,
your arms and legs go everywhere;
the sudden terror in your heart
heard in each troubled breath.
A fish swims in front of you. Then another.
And another. The colours brighter than
the brightest colours in your favourite box of paints.
Now your mouth becomes a gill, limbs
a tail and fins. You drift among reef and fish:
a friend, a fellow fish… until the reef appears
like the living thing it is
to crawl out from the shadows and
seek the light it feeds upon.
Now, caught between coral and the source of light,
fish dreaming turns to fear – you feel the reef
slice into your flesh like a knife, gills
filling with water…

Taking your hand
we find a sand bank
to stand upon, and I explain
how the glass in the mask magnifies the view.
'It changes the look of things,' I say.
'Like the mind does when it dreams.'
Still holding hands we turn
our backs on the reef
and push off for the shore,
floating like lovers on a canvas by Chagall.

4

Legacy

Deliverance

When I feel the need
to push

I pant.
Staccato breaths

arrest (temporarily)
the head

butting the dark,
ease the incumbent

flesh, allay the little
agonies of labour

until the quick,
complete surrender

to the weight of
rushing water. And

like water
like fire

the baby comes –
brutal, cruel,

and simply beautiful.
Then the flames

about the flesh
expire, and the body

bruised and bloodied
lies wasted on the bed,

broken like the husk
of some exotic fruit.

And after being blind
at birth

my mind now wakes
and leaps around the room

yet cannot rest or settle
until it holds the child

like vacuum a void
or fire a fever –

a void
only joy can fill,

a fever
only love assuages.

To her

(A prayer for my daughters)

1.

To her
the setting

of the sun
is like

closing
the eyes.

To her
the dark

becomes
a monster

with hundreds
of heads

and hands
to take

her breath
away.

To her
the night

is cold
as a wet cot

hot as
the sweat

of horses
rearing

at the end
of the bed.

2.

I wipe her brow, hold her hand,
watch her sleep – and think:

perhaps this time she dreams
of foreign fields of green

or a princess waking to a prince's kiss
in some enchanted wood.

For I see no evil, only good,
in this sleeping, dreaming beauty.

Hope that when I whisper in
her ear she will forget her fears

and wake from fevered sleep
to hear herself speak

in a voice as clear and
pure as a poem.

Baudelaire the bricklayer

(After Seamus Heaney's *Follower*)

My father worked like a pack-horse.
Striding the grounds he'd survey the site,
Study detailed plans of the house
To be built, his eye a theodolite.

A bloody perfectionist, he'd cock
His head, calculate the gauge, determine
The bond, and drop a plum-line from the top
Of the frame for square, all the while

Looking like a loony with a knotted
Handkerchief for a hat. But he was no fool.
Once a fresh batch of mortar was knocked
Up, he would reach for his tools.

Now his hands moved through air in time
To conduct the scoop and spread of mud,
The lifting and laying and tapping into line
With a hammer, handle or blade

Of the trowel each and every brick
In the walls he called his 'works of art'. Yet I
Failed to see beauty in stacks of bricks
Or a world in a grain of sand, cement or lime.

The building site was a foreign place
Where men spoke another tongue,
Dressed in ridiculous bib-and-brace
Overalls, and whistled songs out of tune.

I never could wear hobnailed boots,
Or take to digging holes with a spade.
'Maybe you'd be better off in a suit,'
He'd say. 'Or learning another trade.'

So I got through the days by reading Baudelaire
And Rimbaud, drinking absinth, deranging the senses,
Deciding that life is elsewhere
While raking joints and mending fences.

I failed to follow in his footsteps,
Slipped sometimes in my sandshoes
From dodging discarded clinkers, broken batts,
Bricks with double frogs, other nomenclatures.

My father was annoying to work with;
Yapping always, always the verb.
Today his walls still cast a shadow in which
I see a boy awkwardly scrawling his first words.

The bowl

Domestic, the memories of mothers.
Forget the faded photo of a girl
On horseback, the wedding shots –
I wasn't there, and I have moved
Beyond the want of rivalry.
While Dad was always 'in his shed'
Or 'out the back somewhere',
You could be found in the kitchen.
We knew what day it was by what we ate.
Yet now I understand why on some days
You refused to cook, cried, threw cutlery,
And called us a 'pack of bastards'
If we answered or didn't answer back.
Your hysteria took root in the word.

When I visit now it's to find you
On a cold and sunless afternoon
Stooped over the stove ladling soup;
The warmth from the hotplate
Holding you for a moment
Before you turn to show your face…
I take the bowl you offer,
The plate of buttered bread.

Hands

1.

The mother's hands gather
the loose threads of wool

onto her lap. As evening
draws in she finishes knitting

a pullover for her granddaughter.
It will be two sizes too small.

2.

The father's hands are big
and cracked like bricks;

the fingers thick and bent
as planks. When he sits

at the table to wait
for the evening meal

they fidget with the napkin –
still only at the feel of

cutlery, the holding of
the handle of a trowel.

3.

Later that night they turn
off the light. Effortlessly,

each hand finds and takes
the other gently in its grip.

Legacy

for L.R.H.L.

We say they steal our innocence
And leave us nothing in return to show
But guilt. I took my father's shape
Yet do not blame him for the way I look.
They worked their fingers to the bone
To give the best that money could provide.

We like to think we bear the scars
Of uncaring hearts, of hands that struck
In blinding fits of rage. Yet hate
Was seldom on their minds; while love,
It seems, was not endemic of their kind.

Yes, we carry the legacy in our looks
And manners, and in the family name:
A name which in my time at school
Became a popular linguistic game,
A comical nomenclature so often
Misspelled and mispronounced I swore
I'd change to Smith or Jones when I grew up.

For reasons which still remain unclear
You were not seen in those early years
And you taught me nothing that I know.
Then late one autumn afternoon
You walked into my home and showed
Me how to spell and speak my name.

5

Obeying the Call

The path

1.

The path
takes me back
over thirty years
to a time when love
attended my hand
and carved our initials
in wet cement
outside the school grounds:

R L
L
R L

Now I see
a youthful vanity at work
a conceit in knowing
that if she took my name
the letters would remain the same.
Yet I also know
there was the need
to simplify things
make sense of things
set things in their place.

2.

Now the path has gone.
Marked by neglect
the unnecessary tread
of strangers' feet
scrawled obscenities of children
the pavement succumbed
to the blunt edge
of the drill.

3.

Today I stand
on fresh ground
the cement soft to
the touch of my hand.
With studied insouciance
I commence the down-
stroke with
the sharp
end of a
stick.

Ply

for T.

'Ply me with poems,'
You pleaded on the phone.
As if published verse
(For better or worse!)
Can displace our conversations.
As if highly refined lines
Of rhythm and rhyme
Can rival our spoken words.
As if a vexed, complex
Postmodern text
Can eliminate me.
As if a Shakespearian sonnet
With all the seasons in it
Is comparable to thee.

Postmodern blues

Life is first boredom, then fear
– Philip Larkin

Perhaps you'd like to try that opening line
Again because it's obvious from the way
You dress you don't come here often or get
Out much any more. And who can blame you?
Statistics show that even as I speak
Somebody's being stabbed or shot or kicked
To death outside a nightclub not unlike
The one you're in. Still you need to get
Out every now and again don't you? I mean
It does you good. You can't stay home all of
The time now can you even if you do run
The risk of getting in a fight and being hit
And suffering serious injury. Yet there's
More chance of being run down by a car
Or struck by lightning don't you think?
Hey you don't say much do you?

                    Oh, but I do.
Or, at least, I once did. Now, what's the point?
Maybe I was married for too long and have lost
The art of conversation. Maybe the method for pulling chicks
Is different now. My ex now marks the spot and I
Find myself in unfamiliar territory, remembering
A street, a house, and lighted windows at dusk.

By now the dinner party guests
Have fallen to impressions of American sitcoms
(Homer himself hath been observ'd to nod... Doh!)
While the boys at the club are thinking of
Getting down to some serious drinking, being full
Of piss and wind, signifying fuck all.
Oh, our podded lives lead only to the softly spoken
Platitudes of hope... Is that the time?
It seems you no sooner settle into a rhythm
You feel comfortable with when the little separations
Begin. Perhaps I'll try that opening line again sometime –
It might just work the second time around.

On hearing Procol Harum's 'A Whiter Shade of Pale' on 3MP

I'm in a smokeless waiting room
reading an outdated magazine
when it comes on –
after Dean Martin &
before John Denver.
Three songs from three decades:
the 50s, 60s & 70s.
Hip. Groovy. Far out.
I remember when the song
was first released & hearing
about John Lennon sitting in
the back seat of his psychedelic
Rolls Royce smoking a joint
& playing the song
over & over & over…
Then I think maybe
I didn't know about
the incident at the time
but heard it retold by
Paul or George or Ringo
in a Beatles documentary.
When they call my name
I find myself thinking
if only they would change
the station to GOLD FM
then I might hear
that Who song about
hoping to die
before you get old.

Travelling north

Some things in life can take an age to shift, or move
So indiscernibly we never see them disappear from view
Or settle gently into place: continental drift;
A tower leaning by degrees; the migratory flight
Of arthritic refugees who leave to seek an endless summer
Here and eternal skies of blue. Instead they find
Infernal annual heat and ceaseless swarms of flies
In Heaven's waiting room. Still, they seem content to sit
Or stand around at stations or designated locations
And wait for air-conditioned coaches to carry them off
To Dreamworld or into the hinterlands.
                                         At twilight time
The world becomes unreal, or remains too much with them.
So they leave their flats to find comfort in the arms
Of strangers on the dance floors of the RSLs,
(Lest we forget), or draw the blinds and stay inside
With a brandy and TV. Yet, before the last
Strains of 'The Last Waltz' end on a discordant note,
And the final glass is lifted to indifferent lips,
They shall have wearied with age – and in the morning
There will be nobody to remember them. Then they find
Themselves remembering them – the dearly departed, that is –
And, when they do, they understand they have survived
To bear the guilt, regret and grief which memory brings.
For the aching joys of youth have gone, and aching joints
And dizzy spells seem insufficient recompense for all
Those years of married life.
                                 Now, life is nothing more
Than spent emotions recollected in tranquillity,
Induced by Valium and other pills prescribed
By those who say they have their best interests at heart.
Yet, you tell me who really cares about these sad,
Imbecilic, biddable old biddies who spend their final days

And dollars bent over bowling balls or bingo
Tables waiting for their number to come up?
And they do not come up to Paradise for the fruit,
Or because they're fools, or beasts, or blessed – or for a change.
(For they know the more things change, the more they stay the same).
No, they end up here because they have been condemned
For living longer than some, or living longer than others
Would like them to.
                  We only want to live and die
With dignity. I must go now – I think I've outstayed my welcome.

Five haiku for Patrick White

Eyes as blue and deep
as a lake. By dawn a mist
    is on the water.

The earth takes his seed
and yields a tree which flowers
    but does not bear fruit.

Deserts test the faith
of lovers and friends. A crow
    examines the bones.

The ageing heart is
unforgiving, without ruth.
    Pearls cast before swine.

When the circus comes
to town animals desert,
    tents are taken down.

Chrome

It's good to know we still
can look in others' eyes

without desire or envy,
without the risk of losing

your life, the fear
of recognition. Yet,

most of the time we keep
to ourselves: reading;

sleeping; listening to music;
looking out the window

at houses not our own, thinking
of the ones we love –

or nothing at all. So,
when the train pulls in

at Fairfield, nobody takes
any notice. Only when

a can is shaken do we lift
or turn our heads to look

to where the noise is coming
from. Graffiti is writ

then erased by the spray
filling the plastic bags.

Hey, this ain't America, man,
I say to myself. This

is another country, mate.
We do things differently here.

This is Friday
24/03/1995.

This is the 2.07
to Hurstbridge.

At the next station
they get off the train

without having looked at anyone,
without having spoken.

Some shift in their seats,
slowly shaking their heads

in disbelief. Then there are those
who seem to have lost

their place on the page
of the book they are reading.

Comfortable in the knowledge
that the train is not going

to derail, other passengers continue
to sleep or stare into space –

and the silence is killing.

Songs of innocence and experience

I carry the legacy in my looks
 And fashion in my genes
Can read the latest mags and books
 Appear at all the scenes

Attended many private schools
 Can get what money buys
Am taught to win and never lose
 Success the only prize

I'd like to thank my Dad and Mum
 For everything I've got
This lovely house this life of *bon ton*
 This diary for *bon mots*

I carry th' legacy in me looks
 An' fashion in me jeans
Can't read too good ain't got no books
 Get hassled if I'm seen

At twelve they chucked me outta school
 For stealing what money buys
On th' streets ya learn to never lose
 Survival th' only prize

I'd like to thank me Dad and Mum
 For everything I've got
This filthy squat this bag of bon-bons
 This daily bowl o' broth

Café society

for Craig

Back then there was no need to look.
We knew what was written on the blackboard.
The menu never changed:
Spaghetti, fettuccine, and pasta of the day.
On Friday the pasta of the day was gnocchi.
We always ordered gnocchi and two glasses of cleanskin red,
Then began to talk music, football, politics, and poetry.
We have been doing this for more than twenty years.
Today the tradition continues.

Since last Friday our teams have won and lost,
There has been a change of government,
You have released a new CD, and I
Have made more amendments to my manuscript.

Sometimes we get lucky and find a table,
But more often than not we end up sitting on
The stools along the dark timber panel wall
Where the quasi-quattrocento mural
Has been replaced by scenes of still life.
I remember when people shared a table with strangers
Before another bar and bench with mirrors was built.
Either you or I once said the two things were unrelated,
While the other thought it was symptomatic
Of a more widespread malaise in our society.
Over bowls of pasta we lament the changes
To the menu, the liberal increase in prices…
The fact our favourite waiter is gone.

You return to the table with two coffees,
Your tongue having tripped up on
The consonantal minefield of café latte.
In these moments I imagine you on stage
Stammering through The Who's *My Generation*.
Yet your stutter disappears when you sing.
As does mine.
And when you begin to tell me of the ancient belief
That such afflictions were due to the gods
Attempting to speak through the mouths of mortals
We both laugh and agree the gods can only say so much.

Over the years flashier brasseries and bars
Have opened (and closed) in the city's numerous lanes and alleyways,
But we find we prefer the familiarity which breeds content.
We step out onto the street and, before going our different ways
(You toward Parliament House, me to the bookshop),
Agree, as we do every Friday, to meet again the following week
And continue our conversation.

A prize catch

on looks
it seems he'd
rather be
on the river
feeding a line
to fish
than here
feeling like
a fish out
of water
a prize catch
put on show
to satisfy
the tourists
and souvenir hunters
whose questions
search the flesh
like hooks
cameras which
probe the bone
and bloodied heart
while the clear
unblinking eye
looks on

The dream

Our eyes follow the bulging hip
Of the not-so-handsome odalisque
To the clumsy hand and awkward feet
Which belie the artist's grasp of graphics.
We focus on the reclining woman
Because her presence is enigmatic;
But it's the figure of the charming native
(Half hidden in the *paysage exotique*)
And not the naked body of Yadwigha
Which makes the painting so hypnotic.
Et Rousseau? Il s'est cache parmi l'herbe
Behind the red velvet chair playing the comic.
The foliage from a Paris street
He makes a forest of *Afrique.*
Bird beast and flower?
Pastiche of journals on the tropics.

Alice through the looking glass

the car
is mad
as a
march hare
tonight
sleepy
as a
dormouse

the road
ahead
slippery
as treacle

the car
leaves
the road
like a
startled rabbit
stops
like a
soft clock
around
a tree

then
the road
disappears
like a
stranger
into
the dark

and I
step out
of the dark
and into
the light
feeling like
light itself

Idée fixe

for Sylvia Plath

1. Sunrise

Wheel her into the sun –
once she woke to its gentle touch
but today turns her cheek
the other way before light
hits her eyes like a fist.
Discarding her skin, she slips
into a jacket, cocks her head,
and smiles up at the nurses like a reptile.

2. Medication

You were in need of food
    So I gave it to you.
You were in need of a drink
    So I brought it to you.
You were naked
    So I clothed you.
Sick
    So I comforted you.
You were in need of care
    So I anointed your wrists.
You were in need of a name
    So I baptised thee.

3. Rest

the floating world
is seized by images
of dreaming
glaciers
      continents
              drift
are caught
in pale sunlight
a swarm of bees
around a pomegranate
then the bursting of fruit
fleshing forth fish
disgorging tigers
devouring
devouring

4. Discharge

   i am here
out of the flame of love
   hungry and thirsty
out of the centre of the flame of love
   naked
out of the centre the heart the flame of love
   sick and bleeding
out of the dead centre the heart the flame of love
   unnamed
out of the dead centre the heart of darkness the flame of love
   here am I

5. Sunset

In the head the fire
that would not go out
In the belly the baby
that would not be born
O to have emptied the abdomen
unsexed the head
found relief
in bestial oblivion
Then to die like a dog
when you demanded I go
in a blaze of glory
a sunset of knives

Pathetic fallacy

The evening sky is bruised and bloodied. Stars
Prepare to collapse, cars ready for bed.
While the rotary hoist recoils from the coming dark,
The lawnmower sleeps soundly in the garden shed.
Street lights consider retiring for the night
As the house braces itself against the cold.
The fence leans and whispers to the lawn to be quiet,
Wires hum lullabies from telegraph poles.
Inside, a fist unclenches to clutch at a breast;
Outside, a cloud threatens the moon.
He says he hates it when she's obmutescent,
Yet swears her words won't end this poem.
As love is not undone by acts of violence,
The night is not reclaimed with vows of silence.

Remembering Hiroshima

there was a flash like lightning
followed by a roaring silence
and a burst of heat upon the skin
then a barely audible 'boom'
like the sound of distant thunder
i remember waking from one dream
and walking into another
through the blue phosphorescent flames
which flickered like the reels of silent film
like insects trapped in amber the dead
embraced or sat silently at prayer
a woman with a hundred heads was eating air like mad
it was then that i turned away
from the ruins and went to the river
where an animal drifted downstream like an upturned table
so i took the table to ferry people across the river
here the dying would not look at the living
or those wanting to live
and wished that they were dead
while the living felt like dying
yet did not care for those about to die
black rain began to fall and the river forgot to flow
so i stepped off the table and walked across the water
in the distance i could see winged horses rising
from the pools of blood on the ground and seas
springing from the earth at the touch of their hooves

At the kitchen table she sits down and eats

'Mother, mother, my soul's on fire.'
'Yes, dear. Is that a new pimple I see appearing?'
– Elizabeth Smart

She eats by taking a spoon
and shakily sifting the cereal:
leaving raisins, dried fruit and
hardened grains of wheat on the side
of the bowl...like slakeless birds
around Sturt's inland sea.
The house is quiet except for this.
Here, siblings spoilt by untroubled sleep,
The lifeless room downstairs.
It's not the hand that loses touch –
I have to learn to see again.
Still hungry she trusts the knife
and squares the loaf, throwing offcuts
to dark fledglings of doubt.
Defying myth she turns
and looks out to sea, desert
at her back.

Obeying the call

Although the mind has gone to seed
The weathered hands and heart
Obey the call.

It must be hard to break a spell
Of sixty years; a ritual forged
By four generations of men

And borne by every father's son.
How else explain this strange behaviour
So early in the day?

This need to rise before the sun;
Tend the cows; turn the soil;
Or mend a fence

That used to be around here once.
Now, there are nurses to attend to him;
Take him back to bed;

Arrange it so that things return
To normal in this ward; adjust the sheets
To hold him firmly in his place.